OUR HOPE FOR YEARS TO COME

OUR HOPE FOR YEARS TO COME

The Search for Spiritual Sanctuary

Martin Marty and Micah Marty

Augsburg

MINNEAPOLIS

OUR HOPE FOR YEARS TO COME
The Search for Spiritual Sanctuary

Photographs copyright © Micah Marty.

Unless otherwise noted, scripture quotations are from New Revised Standard Version Bible, copyright 1989 Division of Christian Education of the National Council of the Churches of Christ in the United States of America. Used by permission. Scripture quotations on page 87 are from *The Holy Bible, King James Version*, copyright © 1979, 1980, 1982 Thomas Nelson, Inc.

Cover and interior design: Micah Marty
Separations and printing: Gardner Lithograph, Buena Park, California
The Laser Fultone process is a registered trademark of Gardner Lithograph.

Library of Congress Cataloging-in-Publication Data

Marty, Martin E., 1928–
    Our hope for years to come : the search for spiritual sanctuary /
Martin Marty and Micah Marty.
        p.   cm.
    Includes bibliographical references.
    ISBN 0-8066-2836-7
    1. Lent—Meditations. 2. Hymns, English—Devotional use.
3. Hope—Meditations. 4. Church year meditations. 5. Devotional
calendars. 6. Church buildings—Middle West—Pictorial works.
    I. Marty, Micah, 1960–   . II. Title.
    BV85.M363 1995
    242'.34—dc20   95-21440
                                                         CIP

Manufactured in the U.S.A.   AF 9-2836
99   98   97   96   95   1   2   3   4   5   6   7   8   9   10

Author's Introduction

For the next forty-seven days, you and I are going on a pilgrimage of hope, journeying together through stages where hope is promised and where in faith we can respond. To suggest that those of us who page through this book and walk through the days together shall thus come to the end of our pilgrimage and find hope realized would be *outrageous*. It would also deny the nature of hope. It would run explicitly against the belief about hope expressed in the New Testament. There, it is *love*, the love of God in Christ and the love believers get to put to work, that "believes all things, *hopes* all things, endures all things" (1 Corinthians 13:7). There, "*faith* is the assurance of things hoped for, the conviction of things not seen" (Hebrews 11:1).

So faith, like love, has to have its place; without it, there are no reasons for hope. The photographer and the author of these reflections therefore ought to be modest about what we offer in respect to this book and the hope it celebrates. Modest? No, it is hope itself that is *outrageous* and the promises of God that sound outlandish. They want to take over the front of the mind or the surface of the soul, where despair finds its natural place. They want to find their own special spot in the back of the mind or the bottom of the heart, where worry would crowd out faith and love. Finding any reasons for hope requires attentiveness and discipline along the pilgrimage we undertake.

Who are the author and photographer who accompany you and each other on this journey? The author advertises himself as someone who is ending a seventh decade of stumbling and being confused along the way; who often gets saddened and lost; who reads the same newspapers as you and has similar reasons for worry that any person who looks at tomorrow might have. Those are hardly trustworthy credentials.

Yet through it all, I have found that the scriptures we read, the songs we sing, the sanctuaries we visit, and the evidences left by people who designed and built such sanctuaries "for years to come" capture the sense of divine hope. For some, like me, they also represent the familiar, a return to roots.

While doing research for this book, I came across an old file marked "Hymns, E.A.M." In it were papers written decades ago by Emil A. Marty, my father, who was a church organist and teacher. He and my mother instructed their children and instilled in them a love for hymns. Memorized hymns were my father's stock, and thanks to him, now mine. Together with Scripture, they have given and do give reasons for me to affirm, to say yes when the divine promises arrive. They give me confidence to reach out to you with the certainty that forty-seven days from now we shall together be more sure of our hold on the promises of God, the reasons for hope, and the realization of its signals in a setting that we will keep on calling "the real world."

Martin E. Marty

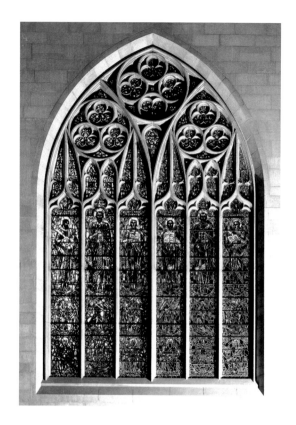

Photographer's Introduction

Why Gothic? Why do all of the photographs in this book depict Gothic churches? Is there some common spiritual thread that links the many variations of churches we call Gothic?

To find the answers, we are about to embark on a visual journey across the United States, a journey that takes us to Gothic worship spaces both great and small. The architectural significance, historical authenticity, and geographic location of these places will not determine our itinerary. Instead, we will focus on a variety of stylistic expressions and seek to discover whether there is indeed a Gothic "spirit."

As a photographer of things religious and spiritual—including sacred spaces, both intended and found ones—I have long been eager to identify what it is about Gothic architecture that embodies and enlivens the human spirit. What perspective do I bring on this voyage of discovery? In photography, as in life, I look for order amidst randomness, and freedom amidst structure; I work to preserve and nurture my own sense of wonder; I seek clarity, simplicity, and awe.

Gothic buildings frequently inspire awe. Every architectural element draws upward not only our eyes but also our hearts, minds, aspirations, and hopes. The medieval cathedral builders strove to focus our attention on things above. It was their goal to capture their idea of heaven in their buildings; it was their way of bearing witness to the light (John 1:8).

We know—as the Gothicists did—that no cathedral can equal the splendor of heaven; indeed, we live in a culture in which we cannot (and probably should not) expend the resources it would take to exactly duplicate the medieval cathedral. But just as composers don't give up creating when they realize they can't match Bach or Mozart, nor painters when they consider Rembrandt or Michelangelo, so too in our sacred spaces and personal lives we can, we should, still strive for new heights. We invest in cathedrals and churches—and sing hymns and pray—for the same reason that we try to love one another, care for the sick, and help the needy: because we know that even though we are not the light, we are called to bear witness to the light.

Our initial question about these photographs—Why Gothic?—is answered every time we encounter one of these worship spaces in person or in print. The cathedral builders—and their twentieth-century descendants—answered the question with forceful conviction. They knew what the Gothic style was about, and we can daily appreciate and celebrate their magnificent expressions. It's about optimism; it's about aspiration; it's about light; it's about hope.

Micah Marty

Brief notes on the photographs can be found on pages 106-110.

9

One Day, One Page,
One Hymn, One Sanctuary

On the pages that follow, you will see pictures of grand and great Gothic cathedrals planned by major architects, often funded by a few people of great means along with great numbers of people with few means. The arches and vaults; windows and doorways; cloisters, stairs, and aisles; niches and carvings were all prepared to suggest sanctuaries for the soul, lasting places in a world of change. We hope you will let these imprint themselves on your mind, one a day, as you face your world of change.

On other pages you will see images of simple, humble art prepared out of wood available on almost treeless prairies. The steeples of these sanctuaries did not have to reach high to express the aspirations of hope since nothing of height challenged them on the plains. These pictures serve just as well for imprinting hope on the mind, one a day, as we reflect on that for which we hope—shelter, love, guidance, . . .

You will also find a hymn stanza paired with each photo and reflection. In our hurried age, with disposable forms of worship and a culture that places little premium on memorizing, many deny themselves the experience of soulful people through the ages. They do not have minds stored with lines of spiritual songs. We want to appeal to those who do have such lines stored away, who can mentally match them with tunes hummed since childhood.

Even more, we would like to win many in a new generation to the comforts and joys that go with sacred songs, sung poetry, psalms, and hymns. Most of the excerpts here can be memorized easily. Or you can think of them as you rest at the end of the day. And you can leave the book open where the picture and the hymn can serve as reminders and, we hope, inspiration for the successive stages of the pilgrimage of hope.

The titles of the reflections can guide the random reader as well as the person who is looking for a topic to match the needs and moods of the day. Read the titles as if they are preceded by "Hope for." Each expresses the theme of its hymn, reflection, photograph, and suggested scripture reading.

Although you will not be misusing this book if you page through it at once or read through it in one day, we believe a pilgrimage of hope prospers most "a day at a time, a page at a time." If you start *Our Hope for Years to Come* on Ash Wednesday, it will come to a climax on Easter. (To help you keep your place during that time, Sundays are marked with an asterisk in "Notes on the Photographs," which begins on page 107.) Or you can start on any Wednesday and you will find that every Sunday the pages connote a corporate act of praise. But pilgrimages of hope begin whenever despair threatens, which is any day, so you can begin here and now, aware of our hope and confidence that such a pilgrimage can be—will be—rewarding.

The names of the hymns and their authors are noted on pages 111–112.

Shelter

O God, our help in ages past,
our hope for years to come,
our shelter from the stormy blast,
and our eternal home.

To hope is to adventure. The finger that turns this passing page, the mind that uses this fleeting moment, the person who wants to hope—all represent elements of adventure. All want to be fulfilled.

To hope is to be human; hoping is part of human nature. But realists speak of hopes neglected or denied. Even worse, we know instances of hopelessness. By definition and in experience, hopelessness is a near equivalent of death.

To hope is not to join the fabled little Pollyanna, whose father had taught her the "glad game." Following its rules, she could convert every negative into a positive. All would then and thus be well. No, we say, not all and not simply so. We often have to play the "sad game" of life, with its different set of rules. The only way to survive it is through hoping.

Those who search for hope, at daybreak before doing or at nightfall before resting, are not completely exposed to forces beyond their control. In a protected corner of every restless soul, there is a sense that hope needs an object, a Thou named God, who sometimes will seem remote and elusive but who has been helpful in times past.

Picture such a soul, on the first stage of a pilgrimage of hope, finding rest under the arched roof of divine care: it will be there for years to come.

Psalm 46

Ressourcement

You are the seeker's sure resource,
of burning love the living source,
protector in the midst of strife,
the Giver and the Lord of life.

The French have a beautiful word for something each of us needs today: *ressourcement.* We do not need to know French to draw upon what the word means. It implies returning to a source, drawing on its depths and richness. The wise ones instruct us to think of sources not as wells or stagnant ponds but as springs and flowing streams.

During our pilgrimage of hope, we seekers will find nothing but spiritual drought unless we reach into profound sources for ressourcement. The soul that is cut from its divine rootage stands no chance to prosper. It will have no nutrients. We cannot go it alone. We set aside some moments each day to reflect on the existence of sanctuaries on the way of life. There pilgrims can retreat and be refreshed. We look at landmarks left by people who went before as they tried to image in wood and stone and glass what eternity itself cannot exhaust: the protecting power of the Lord of life.

The source of such power is "burning love." One would think that whatever burns would die out, leaving only ashes. The last thing we want of a day is ashes. We want and need fire and life and love inexhaustible. Precisely these are promised, sufficient for each day.

John 14:18-27

Love

Spirit of God, descend upon my heart;
wean it from earth, through all its pulses move;
stoop to my weakness, strength to me impart,
and make me love you as I ought to love.

The language of prayer has to be clear, not because the hearer cannot grasp the desire of the vague but hoping heart, but because the one who voices prayer wants to arrange life in the hope that such prayer be fulfilling.

What would it mean to have one's heart weaned from earth? Earth suckles through the food it yields. Earth provides the raw material for shelter and comfort and pleasure. To be weaned from earth might suggest defiance, an arrogant desire for mastery. It need not.

What we hope for today is that defiance and arrogance, marks of being bound to earth rather than being moved by hope, are what would disappear. In their place are to come spiritual, that is, Spirit-derived, impulses moving through our human pulses.

The hopeful human spirit needs to soar, as great arches do; to be translucent and open, as windows can be; to be grounded, as pillars and foundations that provide bases and solidity are. The mortar in all of this structure of spirit, say the voices of all who hope, is love.

"Make me love you as I ought to love you." An aged preacher once admitted that he wished to take back a lifetime of his sermons. "I always had said you've *got* to love God. I had it all wrong. Good news, after Jesus' work, is you *get* to love." We get to love today as we ought to love.

Galatians 5:13-25

Grandeur

Unresting, unhasting, and silent as light,
nor wanting, nor wasting, thou rulest in might;
thy justice like mountains high soaring above
thy clouds which are fountains of goodness and love.

God rules. Those two words can guide us through a day just as they guide us through all of life. The vast majority of the people around us say they believe in God. The moment they or we in our belief or half-belief speak of God, we imply that "God *rules.*"

And "*God* rules." Whatever order we find in our often apparently chaotic universe—and there is some—we must be able to trace back to its origins in the heights, the mountainlike heights of divine justice that presides over all.

Whatever order we find in our often apparently chaotic lives—and there is some—we must also be able to trace back to similar origins in the depths, the fountainlike depths of divine goodness and love. If it is not God's justice and love that are both highest and deepest, then whose are? Then to whom do we trace the glimpses we have of such grandeur?

Such justice does not often come as if with the clap of thunder on the peaks or the roar of currents in the depths. God seems to arrive and be present in quiet ways. Yet the silence we experience does not mean that God is inactive. Where our needs are concerned, God never rests. Nor does such silence imply divine pressure. God takes time and waits for those who hope, waits for them to recognize the signals that come with perfect love.

Isaiah 59:8-21

Awe

For the joy of ear and eye,
for the heart and mind's delight,
for the mystic harmony
linking sense to sound and sight:
Christ, our Lord, to you we raise
this our sacrifice of praise.

A long pilgrimage of hope requires some early stopping places for rest. Along the route of the ordinary experiences that make up so much of our daily lives, we seek rooms for refuge. We need places for retreat since hard climbs and blue Mondays lie ahead.

Sanctuary for the soul takes surprising forms in our postures. A person may lean next to a campfire after sundown or smokefall. Sit near a brook where someone plays praise on a flute. Kneel in a hospital chapel, needing momentary respite from concerns over care. March into a church school classroom where a child parts with a quarter in a collection plate. Rest in a cathedral where . . .

Where tourists may gape and gawk, where sellers may hawk and artists sketch and choirs sing. At such places, after the body has fasted, the eye feasts and for those who have ears to hear, organs roar to drown out the sounds of our stirrings and shufflings.

And after the awe-full roar, the soul welcomes soft sounds of prayer—and silence during divine response to prayer and praise.

1 Kings 8:22-30

Freedom

I bind unto myself today the virtues of the starlit heaven,
the glorious sun's life-giving ray, the whiteness of the moon at even,
the flashing of the lightning free, the whirling wind's tempestuous shocks,
the stable earth, the deep salt sea, around the old eternal rocks.

Along with millions of neighbors around the world, we take up another day's walk in a spiritual pilgrimage, on a journey of soul. We step from the sanctuaries that sometimes shelter us into a world where only technical or money-making activities were supposed to count. Surprisingly, however, people in that world have begun to speak again of soul and spirit. We join them.

To many fellow travelers, the vision of God is not the goal. God is not even necessary to those who speak of themselves as god or of god being the energies in the universe in them. Such contemporaries would reconnect humans with nature. They have reminded us that we are part of the energies of the universe. But connection with nature and energies is finally unrewarding. We need more profound, more enduring ties.

"Binding" ourselves to the virtues of heaven and wind and earth for us means being bound to the one who set and keeps their energies in motion. God is the source and goal who links us with the energies and empowers us. Binding ourselves to this God means being free.

Psalm 139

Silence

I ask no dream, no prophet ecstasies,
no sudden rending of the veil of clay,
no angel visitant, no op'ning skies;
but take the dimness of my soul away.

A companion on the path to hope today is Elijah, who seems to be a strange choice from almost three thousand years ago. He is helpful for his very strangeness. His king called him the "troubler," and his queen was out to kill him. The situation of the prophet was hopeless, so he prayed that he might die. Tired from fleeing, Elijah slept under a broom tree. "Suddenly an angel touched him and said to him, 'Get up and eat.'" Awakened, he was given food there and strength for journeying to the mount of God.

Atop it, he experienced a rock-splitting wind, followed by an earthquake, fire, and then "a sound of sheer silence" in which the Lord spoke to him and gave him a mission, plus the power he needed for it, and then reasons for hope.

Strange and different from our experience, but still helpful, are Elijah and his story. Without any dreams, any ecstasies, opening skies, or angel visitants, we who seek meaning for our missions, the power required for them, and reasons for hope profit on occasion from the "sound of sheer silence." A hinting, barely whispering divine word reveals what we need and crave.

Not fireworks and earthquakes but the sound of sheer silence, now, as then, eliminates the dimness of soul and makes the path bright.

1 Kings 19:1-18

Steadfastness

A thousand ages in your sight
are like an evening gone,
short as the watch that ends the night
before the rising sun.

Some days everything works. One hardly seems to need faith or hope, so rich is love. It is possible on such days to pay the bills and bank a profit; to receive caresses and to embrace; to experience the imagination unleashed and feel creative resources flowing; to be daring. But only the fool is deceived into thinking that life works consistently the way some moments in it do.

In many senses, we are always in training for the kinds of days and moments when nothing works. Life, offering no escape routes, is then a channel down which come occasions for mourning and puzzling contexts for grieving. The people we cherish most died or will die. News of their misfortune or death comes bluntly, and we are unprotected. Our own strong sinews get replaced by atrophied muscles or arthritic joints. Eyes dim and memories fail. Friends betray and enemies prosper. We come to grief, and grieve.

Whether this day, this moment, is a time when grief is a distant ripple or an hour in which it would overwhelm, one constant is clear: a hand described as all-gracious calms the oceans of our tears, warms what was chilled, and will never be withdrawn. That promise is sure.

1 Chronicles 16:7-36

Empathy

Yet I may love thee too, O Lord,
almighty as thou art,
for thou hast stooped to ask of me
the love of my poor heart.

In quest of hope, humans reach *up*, as if our minds were programmed to associate divine rescue with what is out of sight above us. However, the reassuring presence comes from all directions and in all dimensions. In quest of human response, hope reaches *down*, figuratively, as if God were indeed only above and could reach us only by stooping.

The Almighty stooping: this is an image that could seem pathetic or absurd. We ordinarily stoop to enter cars and planes, to reach under the desk to plug in the electric cord, to receive the infant being born. But picture that the creator of universes should be reduced to stooping. Even in our wildest flights of imagination—those scenes in which God gets pictured in human bodily imagery—this one seems most out of character.

Nothing is more *in* character, however, observes the searching heart, than that this Thou should stoop. The doors to our hearts are low and small. How, unless by stooping, shall anyone gain entry? The window on the soul is naturally confined and cramped. To enter it requires bending down. When tempted to reject images such as God stooping as being grotesque, we learn to resist temptation and find that the poor and hungry heart is won to love precisely by a love that bows and scrapes.

Isaiah 53

Covenant

Our midnight is thy smile withdrawn;
our noontide is thy gracious dawn;
our rainbow arch, thy mercy's sign;
all, save the clouds of sin, are thine.

The arch, according to a biblical story, was left as a sign to Noah after the destruction of the flood. It was bowed, as in rainbowed. The rounded arch survives in buildings almost everywhere, but the Gothic artists chose to break it and point it. Never mind, says the admirer of the pointed arch; God graces artists and worshipers under either kind, or both, or neither. Artists leave us with a startling abundance of curving lines, flowing, graceful, gracing.

If a person decides to be picky about styles of arches, she may distance herself from what is on our minds when we use any and all as figures of hope. We use the arch to suggest that the sacred can meet the ordinary and the human can grasp the gifts of the divine.

To be left without hope: that is the terror. The divine smile, if withdrawn, leaves us in darkness. So we want to bring to transactions with the divine whatever it is that we are worth as children of God, what we possess of the dignity of divine creation, as members of the human race that God decided to join in Jesus. But it turns out that we have more reason to hope when we have nothing to bring, nothing on which to have to rely.

Therefore what are brought to the landscape of mercy are only vapors and hazes that obscure the arch, the mercy's sign. At this step along the journey toward hope, the best gift we receive is the breeze that blows the vapors from the scene, leaving nothing but one sign: the mark of unmerited hope.

Genesis 9:8-17

Radiance

When the sun of bliss is beaming
light and love upon my way,
from the cross the radiance streaming
adds more luster to the day.

An author can never anticipate whether any particular page will find readers in an appropriate mood. A photographer captures an image but cannot know in advance whether its spirit will match that of the viewers. This very page may catch the browser in an attitude of deep gloom, against which its talk of radiance and luster will seem cruel. Yet there are reasons to take chances with pages that risk meeting readers in a variety of dispositions. Certain themes are constant, always in place, capable of turning and changing us.

The experiences of writing and reading, photographing and viewing—transactions involved in pages like these—thus match the experiences of every kind of pilgrim along the way. Any of us, bursting with enthusiasm, may intrude upon a scene only to find that expressing exuberance at the moment is thoughtless, in bad taste. Or any of us might crave an inviting or encouraging word only to have insensitive people leave us with discouraging ones.

In either kind of context and in the in-betweens of our regular days, one story serves all purposes. This story about a cross of wood, the cross of Jesus, recalls a day of darkness and earthquake. Those who love that story let it serve just as readily as the sign of a divine radiance. With the gift of love and grace, it brightens the ways, the highly diverse ways, we walk, the courses we must take.

2 Corinthians 4:1-6

Sabbath

Seven whole days, not one in seven, I will praise thee;
in my heart, though not in heaven, I can raise thee.
Small it is, in this poor sort to enroll thee;
e'en eternity's too short to extol thee.

There are times and places when we draw strength by stepping back from our worlds of checkout counters and traffic jams, amusement parks and examining rooms, to retrieve the sacred sense that comes with receiving God-as-Thou, as the truly different other. Every few days—for example, every seven—the pilgrim of hope does well to look both back and ahead. Often this looking occurs in a sanctuary, where extraordinary sights and sounds, thees and thous, invite us to experience the extraordinary.

At best, for many, this other conventionally gets to be greeted on only one in seven days; call it Sabbath. Ever since we moderns invented the weekend, we have tended to separate it from the rest of the week. What happens on the other six days? it is fair to ask.

Today can be one of the "seven whole days" of this week when the soul can participate in the quest for what eternity has to offer. Such quiet participating can seem too brief, too small an activity in a world of stark demands and before the face of a God who wants to be served today in our neighbor. Yet God not only calls doers and prescribes actions but also regards with evident favor the small and poor and almost voiceless. All of which, in different ways, we are as we reflect on the divine ways.

Luke 6:1-12

Recall

*Yet when again in this same world you give us
the joy we had, the brightness of your sun,
we shall remember all the days we lived through,
and our whole life shall then be yours alone.*

A curious thing to say, but philosopher Paul Ricoeur said it: "Hope is the same thing as remembering." That one phrase finds us looking both ways at once. Look ahead, and hope will stare back. Look back, and there, to haunt or to charm, is remembering.

"Hope is the same thing as remembering." We look back at periods of blessed fulfillment, but we also may recall times of unemployment or depression, accidents or losses, and in remembering, may find less reason than before to hope. We look ahead for times of prosperity and a secure life and sometimes find illusion. Visions of utopia and earthly paradise deceive; they never are realized at all.

"Hope is the same thing as remembering." Against all surface logic, there is deep sense in such a saying. Reminiscence, conscious looking back, produces the beginning of hope. It says that we have lived days through with the one who gives joy and sunbrightness in the form of survival. Survival is only the beginning, but we are aware that if we do not survive we do not do anything else either.

Survivors do not tell stories of days in which there were no disappointments or setbacks. Instead they talk about times of trial and testing. Precisely then they found ways of living that assured some sunbright hours amid the darker shadows.

Deuteronomy 26:1-11

36

Victories

And when the strife is fierce, the warfare long,
steals on the ear the distant triumph song,
and hearts are brave again and arms are strong.
Alleluia! Alleluia!

Some days lack plots and are forgettable. Other days—we never know in advance which or when—are filled with conflict and drama.

"The strife is fierce, the warfare long" in the cosmic version of our drama. God and good angels get depicted as fighting the evil angels. Earthlings are not robots or pawns but decisive agents in battle between final good and final evil.

Some people might cart us away if we insisted on speaking of the ordinary irritations and conflicts of an ordinary day as fierce strife and long warfare. Tensions in the workplace, within the family or a circle of friends, may feel so intense, however, that we have to put more energies into them than into our roles in any cosmic, final warfare. Distracting stresses occur on an absurdly smaller scale than that of biblically pictured strife, but they can be consuming.

To trivialize our struggles and strifes would be to do injustice to them. Giving in to small temptations makes giving in to bigger ones easier. On the other hand, recognizing that small triumphs are elements in a larger, clearer plot inspires hope for more victories. We need guidance and signals for such acts. Listen to the heart! From the distance come sounds trumpeting encouragement. They herald reinforcements that are at hand, to be relied upon in our efforts of any day, of *this* day and night.

Ephesians 6:10-18

Wonder

All things bright and beautiful,
all creatures great and small,
all things wise and wonderful,
the Lord God made them all.
Each little flower that opens,
each little bird that sings,
he made their glowing colors,
he made their tiny wings.

On the highest authority we are told that unless we are as little children, the kingdom is not ours. But the pilgrimage of the soul is usually pictured as a desperately adult striving, the discipline of the mature. Wait: do not the breakthrough moments along the way occur at times when we reassume childlike postures and let ourselves wonder?

Back to basics. Back to page one. Back—or forward—to those insights that came with the first little jingles and carols learned before we read, before we ever doubted. The spiritual search produces astonishments when we notice all that jaded experience denies us. The openings of the spirit through which God could be vivid occurred as we watched the squirrels scamper or the birds splash at the bath. We wondered at the mystery of flight and the magic of little creaures. So now: we advance efficiently in our grasps of grace by changing the past tense to the present and letting childlike wonder *now* color experience at our current age. The kingdom is subsequently there for the receiving.

Matthew 18:1-4

Rescue

Stretch forth your hand, our health restore,
and make us rise to fall no more;
oh, let your face upon us shine
and fill the world with love divine.

"I *told* you I was ill!" was the scream that a hypochondriac chose to have carved on his tombstone. Sooner or later ill health afflicts most people. Sooner: there are reasons to look strenuously for health when one is aged, infirm, diseased, or disabled. Later: there will be occasions for everyone to pray for health recovered some day, since few pass through life without some suffering.

For such reasons, prayer for health restored is never only about other people, though sympathetic humans rightfully lift up the needs of others. Midway through a journey of hope, we pilgrims probe our spirits and find other, deeper reasons than bodily ones to seek health. Spiritually everyone stumbles, loses senses, and falls. Soulsickness can stun or numb us any day. If only, if only, we could then rise, because the path is steep and stony.

Authors of ancient Scripture and the moderns who read it have no way of conceiving the divine restorer other than through imaginative comparison to human ways. In such picturing, God stretches forth a hand. That benign presence counters the spiritual malignancies that would destroy the healthy cells of the soul. And when the divine face—picture that—turns to us and shines, love abounds and there is healing.

Luke 5:12-26

Care

Time, like an ever-rolling stream,
bears all our years away;
they fly, forgotten, as a dream
dies at the opening day.

St. Augustine famously said that he always knew what time was until someone asked him. So it is with us. But if we and the dictionary do not know what time *is*, we know what it *does:* it bears our years away.

Of course some incidents, aspects, and effects of the borne-away years remain in memory. Some of us are blighted all our lives by recalled abuse in childhood. Happily, some of us remember being cheered along our way by trophies won or by pats on the back even when we came in fourth. We hear of the death of someone close to us, the birth of a child; a crisis here and a triumph there. These are unforgotten from the flown-away years.

The mind, however, cleans itself of most happenings and most of what had been stored there. Recall an old hotel room number, a license plate on the car ahead of us an hour ago? How we spent a particular April day in a particular year of childhood? Not likely. Dreams delightful and nightmarish slip from the mind when the clock alarm rings; thus do our years get borne away and forgotten.

Is there anything but discomfort in such thoughts that rise in the face of one more slipping-away day? We draw comfort from the context in which we give voice to these: that our years are always lived under "our hope for years to come," which means under God who provides care in the face of the forgettable and unforgettable moments alike.

Psalm 90

Strength

Our hope is in no other save in thee;
our faith is built upon thy promise free;
Lord, give us peace, and make us calm and sure,
that in thy strength we evermore endure.

What good is hope to people who would be left as precarious after its arrival as they had been without it, before they took the first steps in a pilgrimage of hope such as this one? Who would not credibly ask—and expect—calm and sureness to accompany growth in hope?

Artists know how to represent solidity better than they or we know how to experience it. Give builders and carvers piles of stones and time and resources. They can produce pyramids, squat and towering at once—for the dead. They can effect columns and pillars to hold great weights in settings fashioned for praise—on the part of the living.

Knowing the slender hold that most of them have on the weighty and secure aspects of their being, some artists almost slyly punctuate their work with ornaments that can remind those who see them that the artist knows this: even art, though it is designed to outlast our short lives, has its limits. Quakes in the earth tumble castles just as seismic forces—some name them sin and others, doubt—disturb the groundwork of the soul.

The sly signals, however, can be reassuring. Picture a surefooted mountain goat able to endure in dangerous places, where life locates itself, and able to move, just as soulfully each of us must.

Romans 4:13-25

Company

Holy, holy, holy! All the saints adore thee,
casting down their golden crowns around the glassy sea;
cherubim and seraphim falling down before thee,
God everlasting through eternity.

Loneliness is an enemy of hope. The striving person who is alone enjoys limited and dwindling resources for the fight against despondency. Loneliness is an enemy of God, "the first thing which God's eye nam'd not good," poet John Milton said of it. He was thinking about the first page of the Bible and the story there of God's hunger for company.

Hopeful company is not always accessible. In the hospital or prison, in the high-rise apartment or on the remote ranch, and in the midnight hours during our sleeplessness, others are necessarily out of range.

The nearness of helpful company does not depend utterly on anyone's momentary physical environment. The mind is free to recall and to beckon at all times. Poet and executive James Autry writes of an employee who at his retirement banquet spoke lovingly of company founders long gone, of co-workers dead for decades. To the speaker, says Autry, they were as if present. This reality reminded him of what, in his old church in the South, believers had spoken of as "the communion of saints."

Images of the celebrity saints in religious art are often extravagant. Their golden crowns and glassy seas exist beyond ordinary imagining. But the sense of the holy that they and we experience inspirits us today as always and allows us to feel and be less alone.

Isaiah 6:1-8

Constancy

To all, life thou givest, to both great and small;
in all life thou livest, the true life of all;
we blossom and flourish like leaves on the tree,
and wither and perish, but naught changeth thee.

Nothing changes God? Some ancient philosophers decided that if God is perfect, any change in God would have to be toward imperfection. Therefore, they declared, God does not change and change cannot affect God. We can respect those philosophers for their striving to make things come out neatly, but we have this day to live, and their reasoning helps little.

According to the ancient storytellers, the biblical authors, something or some things do change God. The Scriptures tell of one whose mind and actions change when people turn; one who is moved to righteous anger by injustice; one who alters attitudes in order to show mercy instead of divine anger.

Whether over juice or coffee, in front of an open Bible, hurrying to work or resting from it, on a sickbed or fresh from an athletic field, we call to mind the responsive community of those who search in hope. Then we grow less concerned about ancient philosophy and dogma about God's unchange-ability. Aware of the brevity of time as we change, due to the passage of life and our own withering, we have one concern: that nothing will change the character and constancy of God. The power given to us is the true life of the one whose characteristic it is to love—in constancy, in all seasons.

Psalm 103

Peace

Peace in our hearts, our troubled thoughts assuaging,
peace in your Church, where kindred souls are raging,
peace, when the world its endless war is waging,
peace in your heaven.

Through the ages, people of faith and those who build for them have tried to create spaces that connote peacefulness. Even most of those who are casually related to worship, to words of proclamation, to the busy activity charts of worshiping and serving communities, are likely to have stolen independently into an empty chapel or cathedral in the middle of an afternoon to let things happen. The rest of us might be beguiled into such settings.

Among the things that happen in such places—and these are commended to any of us embarked on spiritual explorations—are engagements in acts of recall, which means running through the mental journal of spirit that comes along with memory; enjoyment of the acts of centering, with most worldly distractions gone; attempts to be attentive, to listen for the sounds of sheer silence or to overhear an organist rehearsing for the next day's praise; making resolves.

Far removed, for the moment, is the world of endless wars and, for that matter, also far removed are the elements of the fighting church that could give lessons in cruelty to those who aspire to conflict. But we engage world and church refreshed, after peace has first come to quiet troubled thoughts, and bring fresh resolve and energy.

Ephesians 2:12-21

Glory

You forest leaves so green and tender
that dance for joy in summer air,
you meadow grasses, bright and slender,
you flow'rs so fragrant and so fair,
you live to show God's praise alone.
Join me to make his glory known!

Nature's "dance for joy": it seems precarious and short-lived, a bad risk. The life of leaves and grasses and flowers is bound to disappoint: they die.

Such a reminder is hardly necessary to those whose green thumbs fail them, whose seedlings do not become parts of forests. Who expects cut flowers long to grace the table? A psalm often read at the death of believers is brutally abrupt about grass: it flourishes, then withers.

Both because they are inspired by growing things and in order to preserve the effects of these, painters include flowers in still lifes. Musicians try to capture the dance for joy of the leaves. Carvers try to replicate and thus preserve in stone and wood, in apparently permanent form, the grace of nature. These human creations *will* last thus for years to come, but they too will go.

What remains? Consider the lilies and then consider their creator. Jesus did, and the Sermon on the Mount asks us to. The glory of the lilies passes and they will be thrown into the oven. We "of little faith" are not to worry but to hope in the God who clothes the grass of the field. That is the next step in the adventure we have chosen to undertake.

Jeremiah 17:5-8 and *Matthew 6:25-34*

Depth

As we worship, grant us vision, till your love's revealing light
in its height and depth and greatness dawns upon our quickened sight,
making known the needs and burdens your compassion bids us bear,
stirring us to tireless striving your abundant life to share.

Here comes a direction: enter into your closet, your quiet chamber to pray. Jesus' command to do so applies for some intimate conversations with God about personal needs. But those of us who are by this stage taking seriously the options that go along with hope have our imaginations especially stirred in some of the gatherings for worship. These stirrings often occur in small sanctuaries where words and sounds stimulate and stir readied spirits.

Some builders in every age also provide stimulus by creating great spaces that speak for themselves. We carry pictures of these in the mind, images that urge us to seek new dimensions for hope.

Hope, like love, calls forth "height and depth and greatness." Rendering these dimensions concrete, the giant sanctuaries seem to tell us that we are low and shallow and small. To those who enter or picture them, these buildings offer awe-full invitations.

Awe before the divine: what good does it do in the life of hope? Why seek it? Our times tempt us to regard the other, the different, the Holy One as a chummy equal. But "height and depth and greatness," disclosed by grand use of space and sound, help reduce us to scale. Thus freed, we get to say good-bye, without regret, to the self we had been. It was a self that, clinging to conventional experiences, had been reluctant to hope.

Romans 8:26-39

Foundations

My hope is built on nothing less than Jesus' blood and righteousness;
no merit of my own I claim, but wholly lean on Jesus' name.
On Christ, the solid rock, I stand; all other ground is sinking sand.

Much of the current language of spirituality talks of invisible realities. Its ideas and concepts seem gaseous, abstract. Those who would follow Jesus can walk along part of the way with those who speak such language. But to every one of them there comes a moment when the serious ones want and need something different. Their hopes, our hopes, then relate to someone who has been visible among humans, to very concrete events personified in the one called Christ.

Half the Gospel pictures of Jesus show him being like us: he cries; he tires; he has to go to a place apart to pray. He experiences joys among friends. He also knows suffering.

Another half of the Gospel pictures show Jesus to be strong, solid, often rocklike and dependable. Those who pick up on words of his that warn everyone against building on sand regard him as someone on whom to lean in order to get leverage. As the rock, on whom one can stand, he offers that leverage. On such a claim, believers build hope. On this, and nothing less or more.

In a culture in which the vast majority of the people claim to follow Jesus, it is strange to note how rarely he comes up in spiritual talk. In reality, he grounds it. This day we get to realize something of this claim and we can build on it. The alternative is the sand, the sinking sand, that beguiles and consumes.

Philippians 3:17-21

Presence

I fear no foe, with thee at hand to bless;
ills have no weight, and tears no bitterness.
Where is death's sting? Where, grave, thy victory?
I triumph still, if thou abide with me!

Abide: who uses the word today? "Abiding" has an antique ring. Yet, brought to mind, it suggests comfort and company. A story: On Easter evening, two disciples who had hoped that Jesus would become and remain their helper cherished the surprising company of one who appeared to be a stranger. Would he "abide" with them? In similar situations today, we still ask for Jesus' abiding presence because we live between hope and frustration, in faith and half-faith, with yearning for rest and passion to act.

What haunted those two people long ago and what remains a specter over our doings each day and night is the sting of death. Not being morbid sorts, we can bruskly push it from mind. Experts at finding ways to escape, we turn off the television but then turn it back on, seeking solace in its distractions. We might take long walks, reach out with pleas to others, do anything, anything, to forget or to push away the sense of our end since it seems to abolish reasons for hope.

Yet the abiding presence stays to liberate us if we are mindful. We are now equipped with defiant questions voiced in words from the biblical letter to the Corinthians: where now is the sting of death? Where is the victory that the grave wanted to claim? That one prayer that is never to be denied, one that is available this instant, asks for the abiding presence with us of the one who removed that sting, who shares his victory with us.

1 Corinthians 15:50-58

Praise

Praise to the Lord! Oh, let all that is in me adore him!
All that has life and breath, come now with praises before him!
Let the amen sound from God's people again.
Gladly with praise we adore him!

Retracing the steps of our pilgrimage by paging back or thinking about what has gone before, we are struck by all the connections we have made between hope and praise. Today is a good time to stop taking their links for granted.

Praise usually erupts spontaneously when someone wants to thank God for what has been or to express passion about the now and the here. But how do we praise in the spirit of hope, which means to praise about a future that has not yet occurred? We praise a team for a victory yesterday or a pianist for a performance today but never an athlete for having delivered in the season to come.

On the pilgrimage of hope in the light of God, however, everything is different. Having already weathered days that for many, if not most, include some sorrows and suffering and for all, some disappointments and doubts, are we to be programmed robots who must praise because we are commanded to? If so, why is it natural to praise with "all that is in me," and why ask all the creatures, including plants that have life and beasts that have breath, also to praise?

The long record of praise by people who hope becomes understandable when we recall that what is thereby celebrated is nothing but the character of the God of "God's people," who is steadfast in dealing with us also in the times of disappointment. Hence, we praise.

Psalm 148

Generosity

In scenes exalted or depressed
you are our joy, and you our rest;
your goodness all our hopes shall raise,
adored through all our changing days.

Wrongful hopes—and who has not held them?—deter the seeker from seeing rightful ones fulfilled. That many persons want an enemy to fail is understandable, but some are envious also of friends. "Every time a friend succeeds, I die a little" is the mean confession of novelist Gore Vidal. Preoccupied with such little dyings, a jealous creature has no time for living, for enjoying the good fortune of others.

The ancient prophet Jonah once sulkily hoped that the city of Nineveh would be destroyed even though it had repented. His Lord then overnight produced a castor bean plant. It sheltered the prophet, who exulted in its shade as he looked down, as it were, on the city. The Lord then sent a worm to destroy this giant plant, whereupon Jonah fell into depression and even anger "enough to die." The Lord chided Jonah for being concerned about a bush that lived one day but died the next, while he was unconcerned about the city with its thousands of people to whom the Lord showed mercy.

The acts of hoping for outcomes too cruel or even too petty detract from the opportunities we face this day and this night to be open to goodness whenever it comes—undeserved or unbidden, or even to foil the meager and sometimes foolish plots and plans we invent. That goodness raises hopes wherever it arrives.

Jonah 3–4

Guidance

How gleam thy watch-fires through the night
with never-fainting ray!
How rise thy towers, serene and bright,
to meet the dawning day!

The vision of the city of God has moved pilgrims through the centuries. After all, their walk had to have a goal, as does ours. The vision of God was the final reality, but God was beyond human picturings. The maps for those who rode and trudged toward shrines needed images that matched those on the landscape. For that, a city with its hilltop walls and massive doors, its arches and battlements, lights and towers, filled the mind's eye with beckoning landmarks.

When fog and mist hid the view of the distant city or when the night with its terrors fell, pilgrims might turn confused and wayward, might fail. So in their imaginings, their city of God always had to be lighted, as guardians at the gate kept watch through the dark hours.

On very different sorts of pilgrimage today, it may be in our hours of aloneness that the terror of dark, a terror that can come even at noonday, confuses and threatens. No one walks all the way along the path of hope without having moments when the vision is lost in mist or shadow. But everyone who walks and lets grace light the way is also reassured by the awareness that the fires of those who watch remain lit. The heights where refuge is available are secure. Through the dark hours of the watch, the vision of the city brings serenity and brightness.

Revelation 21

Expression

Lord of all eagerness, Lord of all faith,
whose strong hands were skilled at the plane and the lathe:
be there at our labors, and give us, we pray,
your strength in our hearts, Lord, at the noon of the day.

Writers of spiritual literature often address the beginnings and the ends of days. Even without using the word *I*, their writing may be autobiographical. They project the experiences of their own hearts and souls on others. They may recount their own disappointments and their personal hopes. They rely on the grasp of divine favor they sometimes recognize and then picture how all of this can relate to other seekers.

Dawn, with the breaking of gray light, and dusk, with the drop into darkness, find such authors now fresh, now weary, and thus especially open to the workings of the Spirit. They picture those who read their work also starting or ending their days in the search for God's company, the joy of the divine presence.

What happens during the daylight hours, at the noon of the day? The struggles of life are then most intense. At midday come the frustrations, the waverings and doubts, the weakening of hope. When we experience these, we plunge into work: putting lunch on the table, reattacking the computer, taking a fresh turn at the lathe, reassembling the disassembled pieces of our work, our lives. It takes little imagination in such hours to experience the carpenter Lord eagerly being at our side, informing our human skills with needed divine love.

1 Corinthians 12:4-11

The Cross

When the woes of life o'ertake me,
hopes deceive, and fears annoy,
never shall the cross forsake me;
lo, it glows with peace and joy.

When hopes deceive: this "when"—or "whenever"—disturbs our peace, disrupts the day. Hours move along smoothly as we set forth plans and fuel our actions with hope. But then, as everyone alive knows, this hope can mislead; it can delude those who express it. Hopes deceive.

When such upheaval occurs, however, even the weakest faith, summoned through a wan voice, can cry out that *never* will the cross of Jesus Christ forsake the believer. We note a strange phrasing here, expecting "never will *I* forsake the cross." But this is turned around: "never shall the cross forsake *me*." It is as if the cross were animate, not a something but a someone who will not let me go. In the development of hope, the cross is indeed animate. It stands for the person who will not forsake the believing seeker.

Yet the inanimate cross, the one that lives in the eye of the mind and the tracery of the imagination, also functions in this search. We can compare that object to what psychiatrist D. W. Winnicott called a "transitional object": it is to be employed in "transitional spheres" of life. Children like to use stuffed dolls or blankets during their transits between waking and sleeping, between leaving hope or returning to it. The young outgrow these objects. Never does one outgrow the cross and its story, for they lead to the fulfillment of undeceiving hope.

Philippians 2:1-11

Refreshment

As pants the hart for cooling streams
when heated in the chase,
so longs my soul, O God, for you
and your refreshing grace.

Hope and longing belong together. You long for a return home or for adventure. I long for the presence of my beloved. We long together for justice and peace and a better deal in life. That longing is sometimes quiet, almost passively patient, colored by moods like nostalgia, resonating to the promise of leisurely dreaming.

Sometimes longing is more aggressive. It is nurtured by desperate hunger or thirst, inspired by intense desire. In a cherished biblical picture, the soul dried by need and want craves a cooling stream, just as does a hart, a deer, heated by the chase or dried by the summer's heat, craves a cooling stream. Even city people can easily conjure up remote forest scenes. It takes little imagining for anyone to identify with the posture of the hart, lapping nurture. In this picture, longing becomes fulfillment: at the cooling stream, the heat and the thirst disappear.

So it is with the soul in search of sanctuary and refreshment. What we need and want and are graced to deserve today are not descriptions of streams but the streams themselves; not a description of the divine but the experience of the presence of God. God is not grace and grace is not God, but to the hungry heart and thirsty soul they arrive inevitably in each other's company. And with God and grace, refreshment is at hand.

Psalm 42

Quiet

Drop thy still dews of quietness,
till all our strivings cease;
take from our souls the strain and stress,
and let our ordered lives confess
the beauty of thy peace.

We hear an edge in voices, sometimes in our own. People nearby irritate us with their unreasonable demands. Others scold and pressure us. Tempers flare; virtuosos of rage throw tantrums. Even suppressed anger is revealed, as it makes the vocal chords to sound strained. All these signals are cries for help.

We can often see the signs of stress in our own mirrors. People who are near can cause tension by choosing to be aloof. They force us to be alone when we do not want solitude. Or they are indifferent: their turned backs are forbidding and deathlike. To be ignored is to be made anxious. Fists clench; backs turn rigid; brows furrow. The stressed person cannot be generous or express benign emotions and actions. He, or she, needs relief and release.

Experience tells us that help comes from without. Of course we humans can undertake some disciplines and develop certain techniques to alleviate strain. Stop playing God, the counselor wisely says. Ease up on your schedule. Get a massage and feel less stress for a moment in the day. But sustained help does not rely on passing rearrangements and momentary physical adjustments. We wait in hope for enduring release, the kind promised by the maker of beauty, the giver of peace.

Matthew 14:13-33

Song

Unseal our lips to sing your praise,
our hearts to you in worship raise;
increase our faith, perfect our sight
that we may know your will aright.

On clear nights we gasp at the vault of heavens. On clear days we walk or wheel under it on trails and along fields. Suddenly there comes an impulse to breathe deeply, stare, and turn out both hands to the sky in a gesture of self-offering. We call it praise.

(Those who have never positioned themselves thus to praise might take the hint. Such an action unlocks the self so that hope can enter or be renewed. Today or tomorrow is a good day to enjoy such praise.)

The pause for praise occurs in more consistent measures when people interrupt their walks in order to gather. Dispersing into the world after such gatherings, they, we, can be more ready than before for service in it. Service without prior praise diminishes hope. Without it, we think *we* become the agents of anything that happens and soon come to conclude that an achieved goal, an agenda met, enhances hope for future accomplishments. Not necessarily, for we are frail.

Humans who respond to the one they praise learn to cultivate extravagantly the acts of praising. They build and play great organs and then speak or sing with unsealed lips, uninhibited hearts. All this has one hope-filling intent: to assure that praise fortifies all steps toward hope.

Psalm 40:1-10

Brightness

Lo, on those who dwelt in darkness,
dark as night and deep as death,
broke the light of thy salvation,
breathed thine own life-giving breath.

When a depressed person speaks of hopelessness, if he speaks at all, he may mumble that the future is walled off from him, blocked absolutely. His counselors will recommend radical therapy.

When an anxious person speaks of hopelessness—and who is not on occasion anxious, living at the edge of hopelessness?—she means that the future is dark but a window of possibility remains. She sees obstacles ahead but has not given up hope entirely. Counselors may discern that such a person has focused on too distant, unattainable goals. Focus instead, comes the advice, on what is nearer at hand and realizable, something that builds confidence for the futures that are accessible.

A dying priest retained just enough energy to pass on words about coping. Confessing that he had not enough strength to theorize about prayers or to explain them, he had found enough spirit to pray. "Just do the thing that is ahead of you." That applies in less dire situations, too.

The person of weak faith—and whose faith is not often wavering, plaguing, uncertain?—may live in a conflict dark as night and deep as death. But the window beckons; beyond is the Spirit's air to breathe. The Thou who creates the future breaks through with dawn light enough to guide another day's—*this* day's—thoughts and actions.

Isaiah 9:2-7

Sharing

In sickness, sorrow, want, or care,
each other's burdens help us share;
may we, where help is needed, there
give help as though to you.

Sometimes we can hope for too little and it suffices, if faith is there. One day a leader in an army that was alien to Jesus' people showed concern for his slave and wanted him healed. Jesus immediately promised to come to the scene to help. His presence was more than the military man had hoped for. The centurion pleaded that he and his house and roof were unworthy for such a guest.

Jesus did not go, but he did heal—and praised the faith of the man who asked for help. The sickness of the slave, the sorrow of the soldier, the desire for cure, and the hope of care all came together in this story. It is the kind we still tell to inspire our companions and ourselves to share burdens. If Jesus could go out of his way where help was needed, even among hated alien peoples, it is reasoned, so can we.

So much of the current talk of spirituality inspired by hope is self-centered: *I* must hope and realize *my* hope, which means, have my wishes fulfilled. The Roman army man who doffed his protection and sign of cure, shifts the burden of the search to the plural: *we* discern the need and address it. People with pale and dwindling hopes have only their self-regard on which to trade. When hope includes care for others, the self enlarges, grows generous. The spirit increases.

Matthew 8:5-13

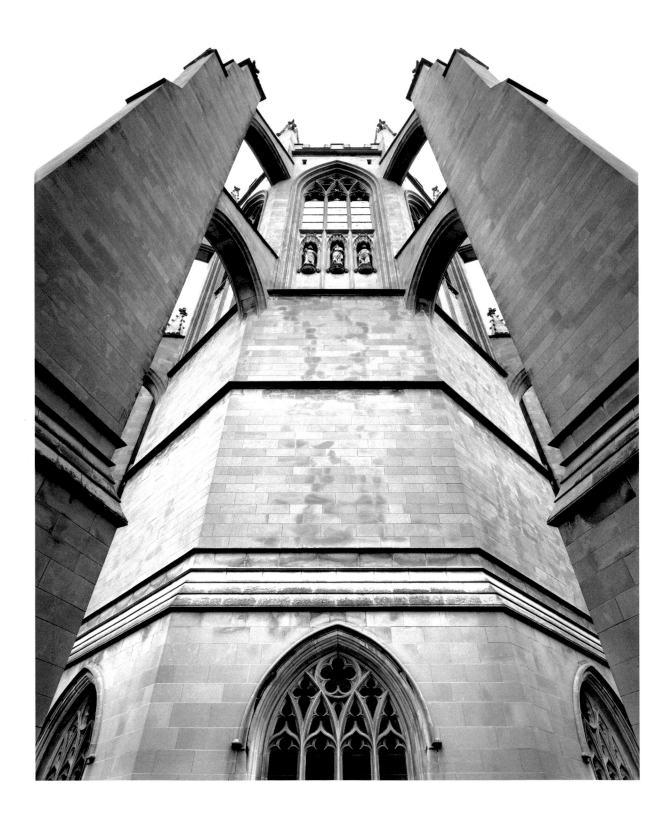

Support

His oath, his covenant, his blood sustain me in the raging flood;
when all supports are washed away, he then is all my hope and stay.
On Christ, the solid rock, I stand; all other ground is sinking sand.

Hope does not equal risk, but it always entails risk. When we hope, we may be tempted to romanticize refuges of the past. In imagination and desire we then flee from the present, the limits of which we have come to know. Hope is risky, because when the futures for which it prepares us arrive, we are so often disappointed by outcomes and by ourselves.

To minimize the risks that come along with hoping, we often fall silent and do not announce hopes. Announce them and we disappoint others whenever our desires fail to be realized. Or we delight those who get ego-satisfaction from seeing dreamers frustrated. To deal with hopes unfulfilled, the wise ones learn to ready a "Plan B," a set of goals that more nearly match the desires and realities of the mature. It becomes evident then that hope cannot be isolated from the rest of life. It needs a balance in common sense that tells us to reckon with and, where possible, savor the present.

Meanwhile, for the sake of risk, we need some solid place to stand, against which to lean, to which to return. Builders create pillars, foundations, and buttresses. For believers, when other supports give out, Christ remains the rock, solid, on which to stand. From whence to dare.

1 Corinthians 3:10-23

Revelation

Mighty and mysterious
in the highest height,
God from everlasting,
very light of light.

A friend whose spouse died tells how he worshiped through the years at her side: "I often prayed intensely. But somehow it always seemed that my prayers got as far as the church ceiling, bumped into it, and bounced back, unheard." Lovers of happy endings would be glad to know that in and after his darkest hours, the friend's experience changed and eventually an awareness of communication with God grew vivid.

This image of prayer rising to a ceiling, however, deserves to be preserved and mulled over by any of us who would also have a vivid awareness of the divine presence who communicates. All thoughtful people know that the depiction of that presence being "above" in mysterious heights, on mountains like Sinai or in the vast and dim cathedrals, is not confining. The divine presence is known as well and as often on the plain, in dugouts and trenches, under the ceilings of bedrooms in huts, or to those who kneel in cramped spaces.

Yet builders who spent decades raising high temple walls and placing windows for day and lighting by night were not exercising futility. Our imaginations need stimulus, and these at times darkly mysterious, at times dazzlingly lit, spaces speak to the soul with the power of revelation. We find respite and, strengthened, walk again.

1 Peter 2:4-9

Comfort

Yea, though I walk in death's dark vale,
yet will I fear no ill;
for thou art with me, and thy rod
and staff me comfort still.

In the emergency room, the stabbed gang leader had enough breath to mock the nurse anesthetist. In turn, she brought up things of the spirit, starkly: "Remember, at this moment I have the power of death or life over you. I want to save you. Don't you have better thoughts?" He mumbled a question: "Do you know the one about the 'still waters'?" They prayed, and he was led "beside the still waters."

Locked in a corner of his mind, perhaps half-remembered from Sunday school in more tender times, was a phrase on which the man could draw. If we know any psalm, it is the twenty-third: "Yea, though I walk through the valley of the shadow of death, I will fear no evil."

The valley of the *shadow* of death is not the same thing as death. Death may come suddenly, soon after a stabbing or more slowly after prolonged illness. But the shadow of death, the reminder that we are finite, haunts any day, every day. Much of the terror of the walk through life towards death results from having to do so alone.

We ask, each of us, "What am I doing today or tomorrow that is more important than being with and listening to the story of someone who fears walking alone?" And as one listens attentively to the other and then speaks, the Thou who is with us will be a more recognized presence who will calm fear.

Psalm 23

Joy

Joyful, joyful we adore thee,
God of glory, Lord of love!
Hearts unfold like flow'rs before thee,
praising thee, their sun above.
Melt the clouds of sin and sadness,
drive the gloom of doubt away.
Giver of immortal gladness,
fill us with the light of day.

Cautious lest we let our hopes soar, only later to see some dashed; bruised because we have been hurt; and realistic because of past setbacks, we quite naturally may be guarded in our emotions.

Then a voice from within us may say, "Be careful about being exuberant, about laughing. If you dance, shuffle; don't leap. If you make music, be muted. Be careful about your pace; you might stumble. Keep your fingers crossed. Being joyful is risky business."

Then a voice from without us will say, "Let go. Let your spirit be released. Sing confidently. Grow flowers and smell and pick and give some. Spin the wheel blithely as you shape a vase. Create delicate traceries and be joyful, joyful."

Not only do we cheat ourselves and those around us if we are only glum or always wary when it comes time to respond to divine stirrings. No, we are then also being simply unfaithful to the surrounding reality. The one who purges gloom has given occasions and reasons, in the midst of life's sadnesses, to be joyful.

Philippians 4:4-9

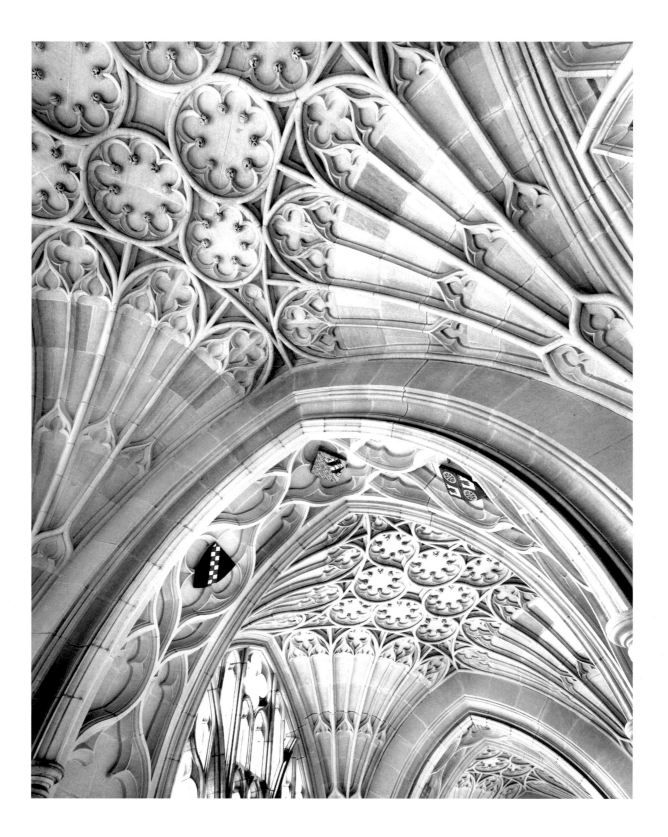

Response

The multitude of pilgrims
with palms before you went.
Our praise and prayer and anthems
before you we present.

What is it about palms that led and leads people to identify them with the coming of royalty? Could it be because their leaves or fronds are broad? Because of that, they wave well, and crowds can suggest a great stir by tearing them off the trees, forming processions, and greeting. In a familiar story that gives Palm Sunday its name, pilgrims to a holy city waved palms to greet Jesus, who they thought and hoped would be their delivering ruler.

The waving of palms was in place, but the popular hopes were too modest. These they identified with something momentary, with another day in the life of a subject people whose history would soon be forgotten. Fixing our minds on the more than momentary, refusing to idolize our own people's temporal agenda, is a more sane alternative strategy.

On our own pilgrimages, be they individual or in company and congregation, we can let palms flourish as images in the mind. Like other such images, they have a purpose. They help us focus on the appropriate kind of greeting for the one whose kingdom, not being "of this world," creates a presence any place. It helps us turn our streets into those of Jerusalem. Along them comes the one who, made present through prayer, works constantly to help us fix on the eternal.

Mark 11:1-10

Immortality

Oh, love, how deep, how broad, how high,
beyond all thought and fantasy,
that God, the Son of God, should take
our mortal form for mortal's sake.

Today we will meet, or will have met, any number of mortals. Unless imprisoned, abed with illness, or confined to aloneness by choice or necessity—in other words, if we are exposed to the social world—we confront a blurring mix of humans. Bewildered, busy, or capable of ignoring most, we find it easy to forget what they represent.

Every one of them will some day disappear, first from our ken and then from this world. The nursing mother already has begun a lifelong sequence of farewells. Many of the people we see wear signs of decrepitude in their posture or skin surfaces. Some faces look abhorrent, for in them we read bodily inscribed records of greed, malice, and madness etched through the years. The surfaces of such bodies and faces and lives suggest that there should be few reasons to want to be part of their experiences.

Then a jarring thought crosses the looking glass of the mind: each of us is one of them. Each belongs to that sometimes noble and dignified but often ignoble and dismaying species called "mortal." After that awareness comes a positive sign: God in the form of the divine Son became a mortal to taste the cup of mortality. The form he took, a body like ours, is familiar. The choice he made thus to become familiar offers dignity to each and all. We live!

Philippians 2:1-13

Access

Just as I am, though tossed about
with many a conflict, many a doubt,
fightings and fears within, without,
O Lamb of God, I come, I come.

We falter during the voyage toward hope when fears, like waves and storms, do their tossing. Blaise Pascal, a voice from three centuries ago, helps pick us up by defining the source of both fear and hope. *True* fear, he says, comes from faith and is joined to hope. Why? Because people "hope in the God in whom they believe." *False* fear is joined to despair, Pascal adds, because people "fear the God in whom they have no belief." That thinker's conclusion: the former fear to *lose* God; the latter fear to *find* God.

The search for reasons to hope, never a simple one, follows a route that can bewilder the conflicted person. That search demands discipline, so it is easy to draw the conclusion that hope is to be found only when one has perfected the discipline and thus deserves to be accepted. However, waiting to hope until perfection has first arrived is to get the sequence wrong. Such waiting frustrates hope and its possibilities. If perfection would arrive, there would no longer be need or reason for hope. Instead, precisely in our imperfection and in our need, we discern the beckonings of hope.

Being tossed about and shaken up, then, are not experiences to be avoided so much as they are to be used. The one called the Lamb of God welcomes us seekers while we are still in conflict and doubt.

1 Timothy 1:12-17

Restoration

Make me to walk in your commands,
'tis a delightful road;
nor let my head or heart or hands
offend against my God.

Facing the day, interrupting it, or reflecting back on it as we may be doing, it would be pleasant to picture that another stage in a pilgrimage of hope has been smooth. Yet almost no day passes without our stumbling over hazards or losing part of the way. In times of setback, we dream of a tomorrow in which to receive fresh directions and commands, new delights and even temptations.

No one can look ahead on the road without knowing that there are not only trivial but also forbidding obstacles, not only insignificant but also drastic occasions when we will lose the way or cause others to. Among these threats, the one that torments is this: that something said or done will offend others and, especially and awfully, will offend against God.

How dire this prospect is becomes clear when we think of the background to the word *offense*. In the Greek world it was *skandalon*, as in our words *scandalous* and *scandalize*. The word referred to something one might trip over or a trap into which one could fall. The expressed hope that no part or action of ours will offend against God does not mean that God would trip or fall. *We* might do that. That is why we seek "a delightful road," along which God picks up the fallen and sets us anew on the way.

Psalm 89:1-15

The Light

We have but faith: we cannot know;
for knowledge is of things we see;
and yet we trust it comes from thee,
a beam in darkness; let it grow.

The mystics talk about "the dark night of the soul" and then about its illumination. The artists who picture subjects conversing with God often illustrate the transaction with a ray of light in the shadows. The agony of Jesus in the garden the night before he died is regularly lightened with a beam signifying the Father's never wholly broken contact. Old "holy cards" portrayed saints in cells or wards or prisons, never abandoned because a shaft of divine light breaks in.

Such light is a symbol, *only* a symbol we like to say. But in Scripture and among the ancients, it was not inappropriate to say "God is light," which is not the same as saying "light is God." God is the light of knowledge of the sort that comes with faith and hope and love. The disciples who slept while Jesus prayed and agonized in the garden were people to whom faith did not come easily. They could doze and be indifferent and get things wrong. But in the shadows of trees in the gardens where they struggled to stay awake and in the gloom of darkness where we struggle to know the path, knowledge of God breaks in with light, as light, *the* light.

Matthew 26:6-46

Language

What language shall I borrow to thank thee, dearest friend,
for this thy dying sorrow, thy pity without end?
Oh, make me thine forever, and should I fainting be,
Lord, let me never, never outlive my love to thee.

The language of thanks is not natural. Speaking words of gratitude is learned behavior: "Say thanks, child!" The president of the United States has to proclaim Thanksgiving Day to an otherwise distracted and self-preoccupied nation.

The language of thanks to a savior who is called a friend is also not natural. We would rather rescue ourselves, without any help. Most counsel we receive urges that we should take control of our lives, assume mastery, and then dominate ourselves and situations. To thank a savior, a friend, a rescuer, means to go beyond what is natural and to have to borrow a language.

Which one? Now the language of self-help manuals is unhelpful. How-to advice books will not show us how to be delivered into freedom. They leave us with only our own resources.

What language shall we borrow? Here the word of hope merges with the word of thanks. We learn it from the one who, on the cross, still addressed the Father, who provides speech that lifts us from silence and despair to the sphere where love inexhaustible will fulfill our hopes.

Mark 15:22-39

Reassurance

Christ leads me through no darker room
than he went through before;
all who into God's kingdom come
must enter by that door.

Children hope for what is on the other side of one door, where the birthday presents or surprise guests have been hidden. There are also doors of opportunity that lure us as we pursue careers and enterprises. And when yet other doors open, homecomings and reunions occur.

Doors also represent the threat of an end to hopes. They get slammed when marriages fail, when children are disowned, when conquerors drive exiles away, when love goes. We look at a door in our own abode and let imagination work to recall all that has passed through it.

We also picture a door beyond which taunters pushed a plait of thorns on Jesus' head and lashed that condemned person's back.

Dark rooms beyond heavy doors portend uncertainties, hazards that threaten to be so menacing that hope cannot survive. To be told that those who are marked by his name and are to be led by Christ through the kind of doors he opened and entered is partly reassuring. The lure that adds to the reassurance is the promise of life in the kingdom, which means wherever God is seen to be active. If we follow, we find that the dark room is lightened now by the presence of the one who has entered it just ahead.

Mark 15:40-47

Newness

A new creation comes to life and grows
as Christ's new body takes on flesh and blood.
The universe restored and whole will sing:
Hallelujah!

The pilgrims of hope find temporary refuges, sanctuaries along the way. Yet the longer they live, the more likely they are also ready to agree with the medieval sages who said that there is no stopping place. Nor was there ever, because the one who said "I am the way" has created for them, for us, a way more than a retreat. Proclaimed as arisen from death, this Lord of the way invites the careworn to be refreshed, indeed to experience new life.

So there are times when one looks ahead with fresh perspective, not only when hopes have been frustrated but also when they have been partly realized. The pilgrim looks: it is as if one has climbed high on the mountain but sees much more is ahead. The stones on the immediate path look like the stones traversed below. The stream is the same, though now one is nearer the headwaters. What is new is perspective: the traveler can look down to the plain where the climb began, to the lower trees that once towered but that, from new heights, appear to have shrunk. And portentously, as night falls, one sees the shadow of the mountain falling on the distant fields below.

This perspective comes with faith and hope as these begin to be realized. But more than mere perspective is here. A new reality replaces the old. A new creation has come to life. And we are bidden to be new beings, readied for the next walk, the next adventures, a continuing pilgrimage of hope.

2 Corinthians 5:1-17

The Photographs

There were two primary challenges in photographing this book. The first, discussed in the photographer's introduction, was to see the light, to identify a common thread in disparate Gothic worship spaces. The second was to bear witness to that light, to capture it photographically and to convey it to the reader.

The medium for capturing the spirit of Gothic was never in question. Because it allows more room for interpretation, black-and-white can be more expressive than color photography. In other words, while color may be better at showing exactly what something looks like, it often cannot match black-and-white for conveying what a subject *feels* like.

Choosing the subjects was considerably more difficult. Even limiting the book to Gothic churches didn't narrow it very much: there are tens of thousands of Gothic worship spaces in the United States. Of course some are truer to medieval ideals than are others, as students of architecture are quick to point out with their checklists that measure just how Gothic a building is. A few elements are always present (the pointed arch and window). Others are expected but not required (colorful stained glass; elaborate carving and detail in stone and wood; soaring external buttresses to support high, thin walls; particular combinations of ribs and vaulting to support the ceiling and roof).

In this book, the overall effect of Gothic is more important than the sum of its architectural parts. My goal as photographer, therefore, was to capture and convey the feeling of Gothic rather than dispassionately catalog its ingredients. What matters here is whether those elements combine to produce a feeling of celestial lightness and awe-inspiring majesty, goals of Gothicists from the twelfth century to the present.

In choosing subjects, I focused on what might be called the golden age of American Gothic, a period during which the quantity and quality of Gothic religious expression on this continent exceeded that of any time in American history. Lasting about a half-century, roughly from 1890 to 1940, this golden age saw the construction of numerous stone churches and cathedrals that are as true to medieval cathedrals as one could hope to build in the modern age. Often erected by large urban congregations or dioceses that had the resources to create "true" Gothic scale and detail, these buildings will long stand as testimony to the perseverance of religion in what many had predicted would be a fairly secular century.

To counterbalance these expressions of American High Gothic, I also photographed modest wood-frame churches on the Great Plains. In many cases, the only things Gothic about these humble structures are a trio of pointed windows and a matching arch over the front door. Still, the hardy pioneers who gathered to build these simple churches probably held many of the

The Photographs

same aspirations as did their European counterparts who pooled *their* talents to build Gothic churches in small villages almost eight centuries before.

That this enduring spirit can be found in Gothic churches from California to New England confirms that there is an undeniably consistent thread unique to this architectural style. It also refutes the criticism that only 800-year-old Gothic is genuine: these modern interpretations of a medieval idiom clearly derive their strength—as does religion itself—from the ability to find new expressions without abandoning a sense of tradition and timelessness.

—Micah Marty

Notes on the Photographs

Cover – The journey, not only the destination, invites and intrigues us. (St. George's Chapel, Middletown, Rhode Island)

Frontispiece *(page 2)* – Spiral stairs, winding their way up into a tower, promise a view from the top as well as lookouts along the way. (St. George's Chapel, Middletown, Rhode Island)

Author's Introduction *(page 6)* – An identifying feature of Gothic—the pointed window—can be found even in the most humble prairie churches. (Platte County, Nebraska)

Photographer's Introduction *(page 8)* – Stained-glass windows developed into an elaborate art form in the Middle Ages, when cathedral-goers without access to the written word relied on visual imagery to tell the stories of the Bible. (Fourth Presbyterian Church, Chicago)

One Day, One Page *(page 10)* – Our life's journey unfolds day by day, revealing many angles, many opportunities. (Washington National Cathedral, Washington, D.C.)

Shelter *(page 13)* – When we rest under Gothic pillars and vaults—often likened to a grove of tall trees—we take comfort from an almost instinctual sense of shelter. (Washington National Cathedral, Washington, D.C.)

Ressourcement *(page 14)* – Seeking serenity and quiet, we retreat to the back of the balcony and kneel in prayer. (Colfax County, Nebraska)

Love *(page 17)* – We don't need to see the source of the light to experience its intensity. (Washington National Cathedral, Washington, D.C.)

Grandeur *(page 18)* – Cathedrals remind us of both our potential and our insignificance, of how high we can reach and how small we are. (Cathedral Church of St. John the Divine, New York)

*Awe *(page 21)* – In Gothic, the primary emphasis is the vertical—lifting our hearts and minds to things above. (Washington National Cathedral, Washington, D.C.)

*Asterisks mark Sundays for those who choose to begin this journey on Ash Wednesday and follow it through Lent

The Photographs

Freedom *(page 22)* – This abandoned Gothic church—like a once-proud ship on the prairie—retains its imposing form even though its details have been stripped. (Webster County, Nebraska)

Silence *(page 25)* – Although largely unnoticed many stories above worshipers, carved ceiling bosses—at the intersection of vaults—show remarkable attention to detail. (Washington National Cathedral, Washington, D.C.)

Steadfastness *(page 26)* – Taking literally Jesus' words "On this rock I will build my church," we date and dedicate cornerstones with great ceremony, making their crumbling all the more poignant. (Adams County, Nebraska)

Empathy *(page 29)* – Solitude emphasizes the vastness of a Gothic worship space built for the throngs. (Princeton University Chapel, Princeton, New Jersey)

Covenant *(page 30)* – Comforted by the protection of arches above and invited by the light ahead, we are given courage for our journey. (Washington National Cathedral, Washington, D.C.)

Radiance *(page 33)* – Even when seemingly overshadowed by the world around it, the cross stands out in the darkness. (Grace Cathedral, San Francisco)

*Sabbath *(page 34)* – The most meaningful events and celebrations, the comings and goings of life, often occur in ordinary spaces that become extraordinary because we set them apart. (Cuming County, Nebraska)

Recall *(page 37)* – We remember not just the milestones and monuments of our lives but also that which we commit to memory through everyday use and wear. (Madison County, Nebraska)

Victories *(page 38)* – The organ pipes echo the stone columns, drawing us up to hear the angel's triumphant song. (Princeton University Chapel, Princeton, New Jersey)

Wonder *(page 41)* – Even in the pre-dawn light, gardens reflect the wonder of creation. (Washington National Cathedral, Washington, D.C.)

Rescue *(page 42)* – The cowering figures on this carved pew end remind us that we all know fear and anxiety. (Washington National Cathedral, Washington, D.C.)

Care *(page 45)* – Memory is the surest way to hold onto elusive moments that are as fleeting as a sunrise. (Seward County, Nebraska)

Strength *(page 46)* – Stonecarvers express not only the weighty but the fanciful, in this case perching a mountain goat on the edge of an indoor abyss. (Washington National Cathedral, Washington, D.C.)

*Company *(page 49)* – The two doorways at the base of this breathtaking reredos give us a sense of scale. (St. Thomas Church on Fifth Avenue, New York)

Constancy *(page 50)* – With each new season, we find new harmonies between the natural and the human-made. (St. George's Chapel, Middletown, Rhode Island)

Peace *(page 53)* – Although relegated to the back row of the church, the old handcrafted pew retains its dignity. (Platte County, Nebraska; image is reversed)

Glory *(page 54)* – In the swaying grasses we feel the ebb and flow of life; we perceive nature rising to reclaim what our forebears intended to be permanent. (Seward County, Nebraska)

Depth *(page 57)* – We often think of depths as something to which we sink—as that which is beneath us—but from a loftier perspective we can see our own position as the depths of a more majestic view. From any position, we remain in the shadow of the cross. (Washington National Cathedral, Washington, D.C.)

The Photographs

Foundations (*page 58*) – We often take pillars for granted, not noticing the subtle marks of the stonecutters' labor. (Princeton University Chapel, Princeton, New Jersey)

Presence (*page 61*) – When we see the solitary church and cemetery beneath the turbulent sky, we are struck by the faith of those who settled the prairie. (Colfax County, Nebraska)

*Praise (*page 62*) – Fanfare, celebration, and praise are not confined to orderly expression but burst forth with exuberance. (Princeton University Chapel, Princeton, New Jersey)

Generosity (*page 65*) – In Gothic cathedrals, the myriad small details—such as this carving of Jonah—combine to tell the larger story. (Washington National Cathedral, Washington, D.C.)

Guidance (*page 66*) – At the edges of the day—when we're not sure whether it's day or night—a light shows the way. (Washington National Cathedral, Washington, D.C.)

Expression (*page 69*) – An organ builder's scrap pile illustrates that what may appear to one person as chaos and hopelessness may well be to another, order and potential. (Washington National Cathedral, Washington, D.C.)

The Cross (*page 70*) – Under close scrutiny, the complexity and angles of a Gothic chancel reveal many crosses. (Washington National Cathedral, Washington, D.C.; image is reversed)

Refreshment (*page 73*) – The splashing and gurgling of the fountain remind us of the promise of life-giving water. (Washington National Cathedral, Washington, D.C.)

Quiet (*page 74*) – Although we think of fog as something that clouds or obscures, it can also reduce objects to their basic form, thus clarifying their essence. (York County, Nebraska)

*Song (*page 77*) – Each pipe contributes its own unique voice to the organ's mighty song of praise. (Rockefeller Chapel, University of Chicago)

Brightness (*page 78*) – A lone window in a dark church leads us to wonder whether windows are to let light in or imaginations out. (Webster County, Nebraska)

Sharing (*page 81*) – Biblical accounts are given dimension by artists' representations. (Washington National Cathedral, Washington, D.C.)

Support (*page 82*) – As medieval cathedrals soared to unprecedented heights, builders introduced massive buttresses to support the sheer walls. (Washington National Cathedral, Washington, D.C.)

Revelation (*page 85*) – The interwoven vaults reveal the skeletal structure of the cathedral ceiling. (Washington National Cathedral, Washington, D.C.)

Comfort (*page 86*) – The numbers for the church hymnboard represent the familiar hymns and verses through which we express and experience our faith. (Cuming County, Nebraska)

Joy (*page 89*) – Joy finds its expression in dizzying motion and exuberant energy. (St. George's Chapel, Middletown, Rhode Island)

*Response (*page 90*) – Abstract depictions of flowers and trees—like these palms—are frequently found in Gothic carving. (Washington National Cathedral, Washington, D.C.)

Immortality (*page 93*) – Built to last but showing their age: the tombstones echo the steeple and windows of the weathered church. (Nemaha County, Nebraska)

The Photographs

Access *(page 94)* – Along our journeys, we encounter places for climbing, meandering, waiting. (Washington National Cathedral, Washington, D.C.)

Restoration *(page 97)* – We quietly reflect on our pilgrimage as we prepare to enter the sanctuary. (Greeley County, Nebraska)

The Light *(page 98)* – Hope is not lost in the shadows when there are reminders of the light in which we trust. (Washington National Cathedral, Washington, D.C.)

Language *(page 101)* – The magnitude of the sacrifice is made more profound in the recounting of being spat upon and abandoned on the cross. (Webster County, Nebraska)

Reassurance *(page 102)* – We hold before us, through life's passages, the image of the cross, the promise and presence of Christ. (Washington National Cathedral, Washington, D.C.)

*Newness *(page 105)* – As we begin a new stage in our journey, we look to the future with hope. (Princeton University Chapel, Princeton, New Jersey)

Technical Notes

For maximum clarity, the photographs were made with a traditional bellows-equipped view camera (see back cover), utilizing lenses ranging from 150 mm to 600 mm (equivalent to roughly 20 mm and 80 mm in 35 mm format). The resulting 8" x 10" negatives are about the size of these pages, so most of the reproductions in this book have actually been reduced rather than enlarged. In a few cases, when quarters were tight or a long telephoto lens was called for, medium format (6x7cm and 6x9cm) cameras were employed and the negatives were enlarged as appropriate.

The Hymns

Hymn stanzas are listed alphabetically by first line. Each entry includes the name of the hymn and its author.

"A new creation comes to life and grows" (*page 104*) – By John B. Geyer, b. 1932, alt. Copyright © John B. Geyer. Used by permission. From "We Know That Christ Is Raised."

"A thousand ages in your sight" (*page 27*) – By Isaac Watts, 1674–1748, alt. From "O God, Our Help in Ages Past."

"All things bright and beautiful" (*page 40*) – By Cecil. F. Alexander, 1818–1895. From "All Things Bright and Beautiful."

"And when the strife is fierce, the warfare long" (*page 39*) – By William W. How, 1823–1897, alt. From "For All the Saints."

"As pants the hart for cooling streams" (*page 72*) – By Nahum Tate, 1652–1715; Nicholas Brady, 1659–1726, alt. From "As Pants the Hart for Cooling Streams."

"As we worship, grant us vision" (*page 56*) – By Albert F. Bayly, 1901–1984, alt. Copyright © Oxford University Press. Used by permission. From "Lord, Whose Love in Humble Service."

"Christ leads me through no darker room" (*page 103*) – By Richard Baxter, 1615–1691. From "Lord, It Is in Thy Tender Care."

"Drop thy still dews of quietness" (*page 75*) – By John G. Whittier, 1807–1892. From "Dear Lord and Father of Mankind."

"For the joy of ear and eye" (*page 20*) – By Folliott S. Pierpoint, 1835–1917, alt. From "For the Beauty of the Earth."

"His oath, his covenant, his blood" (*page 83*) – By Edward Mote, 1797–1874, alt. From "My Hope Is Built on Nothing Less."

"Holy, holy, holy! All the saints adore thee" (*page 48*) – By Reginald Heber, 1783–1826, alt. From "Holy, Holy, Holy."

"How gleam thy watch-fires through the night" (*page 67*) – By Samuel Johnson, 1822–1882. From "City of God, How Broad and Far."

"I ask no dream, no prophet ecstasies" (*page 24*) – By George Croly, 1780–1860. From "Spirit of God, Descend upon My Heart."

"I bind unto myself today the virtues of the starlit heaven" (*page 23*) – Attr. St. Patrick, c. 372–466; para. Cecil F. Alexander, 1818–1895. From "I Bind unto Myself Today."

"I fear no foe, with thee at hand to bless" (*page 60*) – By Henry F. Lyte, 1793–1847. From "Abide with Me."

"In scenes exalted or depressed" (*page 64*) – By Philip Doddridge, 1702–1751. From "Great God, We Sing That Mighty Hand."

"In sickness, sorrow, want, or care" (*page 80*) – By Godfrey Thring, 1823–1903, alt. From "O God of Mercy, God of Light."

"Joyful, joyful we adore thee" (*page 88*) – By Henry Van Dyke, 1852–1933. From "Joyful, Joyful We Adore Thee."

"Just as I am, though tossed about" (*page 95*) – By Charlotte Elliott, 1789–1871. From "Just as I Am, without One Plea."

"Lo, on those who dwelt in darkness" (*page 79*) – By Martin H. Franzmann, 1907–1976. Copyright © 1969 Concordia Publishing House. Used by permission. From "Thy Strong Word."

"Lord of all eagerness, Lord of all faith" (*page 68*) – By Jan Struther, 1901–1953. From *Enlarged Songs of Praise*, 1931. Used by permission of Oxford University Press. From "Lord of All Hopefulness."

"Make me to walk in your commands" (*page 96*) – By Isaac Watts, 1674–1748, alt. From "Oh, That the Lord Would Guide My Ways."

"Mighty and mysterious in the highest height" (*page 84*) – By Caroline Maria Noel, 1817–1877. From "At the Name of Jesus."

"My hope is built on nothing less" (*page 59*) – By Edward Mote, 1797–1874, alt. From "My Hope Is Built on Nothing Less."

"O God, our help in ages past" (*page 12*) – By Isaac Watts, 1674–1748, alt. From "O God, Our Help in Ages Past."

"Oh, love, how deep, how broad, how high" (*page 92*) – Attr. Thomas á Kempis, 1380–1471; tr. Benjamin Webb, 1819–1885, alt. From "Oh, Love, How Deep."

"Our hope is in no other save in thee" (*page 47*) – Attrib. to John Calvin, 1509–1564; tr. Elizabeth Lee Smith, 1817–1898, alt. From "I Greet Thee, Who My Sure Redeemer Art."

"Our midnight is thy smile withdrawn" (*page 31*) – By Oliver Wendell Holmes, 1809–1894. From "Lord of All Being."

"Peace in our hearts, our troubled thoughts assuaging" (*page 52*) – By Matthäus A. von Löwenstern, 1594–1648; tr. Philip Pusey, 1799–1855. From "Lord of Our Life."

"Praise to the Lord! Oh, let all that is in me adore him!" (*page 63*) – By Joachim Neander, 1650–1680; tr. Catherine Winkworth, 1829–1878, alt. From "Praise to the Lord, the Almighty."

"Seven whole days, not one in seven" (*page 35*) – By George Herbert, 1593–1633. From "King of Glory, King of Peace."

"Spirit of God, descend upon my heart" (*page 16*) – By George Croly, 1780–1860. From "Spirit of God, Descend upon My Heart."

"Stretch forth your hand, our health restore" (*page 43*) – By Charles Coffin, 1676–1749; tr. composite. From "On Jordan's Banks the Baptist's Cry."

The Hymns

"The multitude of pilgrims" *(page 91)* – By Theodulph of Orleans, c. 760–821; tr. John M. Neale, 1818–1866, alt. From "All Glory, Laud, and Honor."

"Time, like an ever-rolling stream" *(page 44)* – By Isaac Watts, 1674–1748, alt. From "O God, Our Help in Ages Past."

"To all, life thou givest, to both great and small" *(page 51)* – By W. Chalmers Smith, 1824–1908, alt. From "Immortal, Invisible, God Only Wise."

"Unresting, unhasting, and silent as light" *(page 19)* – By W. Chalmers Smith, 1824–1908, alt. From "Immortal, Invisible, God Only Wise."

"Unseal our lips to sing your praise" *(page 76)* – By Wilhelm II, 1598–1662; tr. Catherine Winkworth, 1829–1878, alt. From "Lord Jesus Christ, Be Present Now."

"We have but faith: we cannot know" *(page 99)* – By Alfred Tennyson, 1802–1892. From "Strong Son of God, Immortal Love."

"What language shall I borrow" *(page 100)* – Attr. Bernard of Clairvaux, 1091–1153; Paul Gerhardt, 1607–1676; tr. James W. Alexander, 1804–1859. From "O Sacred Head, Now Wounded."

"When the sun of bliss is beaming" *(page 32)* – By John Bowring, 1792–1872. From "In the Cross of Christ I Glory."

"When the woes of life o'ertake me" *(page 71)* – By John Bowring, 1792–1872. From "In the Cross of Christ I Glory."

"Yea, though I walk in death's dark vale" *(page 87)* – *Psalter*, Edinburgh, 1650. From "The Lord's My Shepherd."

"Yet I may love thee too, O Lord" *(page 28)* – By Frederick W. Faber, 1814–1863. From "My God, How Wonderful Thou Art."

"Yet when again in this same world you give us" *(page 36)* – By Dietrich Bonhoeffer, 1906–1945; tr. Fred Pratt Green, b. 1903. Translation copyright © 1974 Hope Publishing Co., Carol Stream, IL 60188. All rights reserved. Used by permission. From "By Gracious Powers."

"You are the seeker's sure resource" *(page 15)* – Medieval, ninth or tenth century; tr. John Webster Grant. Copyright © John Webster Grant. Used by permission. From "O Holy Spirit, by Whose Breath."

"You forest leaves so green and tender" *(page 55)* – By Johann Mentzer, 1658–1734; tr. *The Lutheran Hymnal*, 1941, alt. From "Oh, That I Had a Thousand Voices."

Acknowledgments

Behind the scenes during the production of any work as complex as this book, there are frequently individuals whose name does not appear on the title page but very well could. In this case, Ann Rehfeldt is that person. With the photographer, author, and publisher often thousands of miles apart, Ann adroitly coordinated the work of all three and served as editor of every line. She has been reticent about being singled out for special gratitude, but we could not in good conscience go to press without recognizing her, and all who use this book will benefit from her considerable talents and efforts. During the year of its production, Ann regularly mentioned that just as the author and photographer were using the book to advance their own spiritual journeys, so too her participation enhanced her pilgrimage. We appreciate the fact that we have grown together and look forward to future collaborations.

The photographer is grateful for those who smoothed the way and helped provide access to the worship spaces pictured here. Some of the people who went out of their way include William Bryant Logan and Cynthia Yoder at the Cathedral Church of St. John the Divine in New York; Morgan Holman at St. Thomas Church on Fifth Avenue in New York; Robert Becker, Susan Harrison, and the delightful volunteers at Washington National Cathedral in Washington, D.C.; David Chewning, Justin Harmon, and Gary Hill at Princeton University in Princeton, New Jersey; Susan Erdey at St. George's School in Middletown, Rhode Island; Marcella and Robert Dvorak and Emil and Emma Jedlicka of Colfax County, Nebraska; Wallace and Elaine Kelberlau of Cuming County, Nebraska; Amelia Schmertz of Rockefeller Chapel at the University of Chicago; and John Buchanan, Don Hagerty, and Bob Rasmussen at the Fourth Presbyterian Church of Chicago. Also, special thanks to Karen Thomas in Washington, Mary DeNadai in Philadelphia, Brian O'Connell in New York, and David Murphy of the Nebraska State Historical Society for their generosity and assistance.